FORTUNE
FAVOURS
THE
Bold

summersdale

FORTUNE FAVOURS THE BOLD

Summersdale Publishers Ltd
46 West Street
Chichester
West Sussex
PO19 1RP
UK

www.summersdale.com

Printed and bound in the Czech Republic

ISBN: 978-1-84953-888-6

Substantial discounts on bulk quantities of Summersdale books are available to corporations, professional associations and other organisations. For details contact Nicky Douglas by telephone: +44 (0) 1243 756902, fax: +44 (0) 1243 786300 or email: nicky@summersdale.com.

Make your
dreams a reality

NOTHING IS IMPOSSIBLE; THE WORD ITSELF SAYS 'I'M POSSIBLE'!

Audrey Hepburn

PATIENCE AND PERSEVERANCE HAVE A MAGICAL EFFECT BEFORE WHICH DIFFICULTIES DISAPPEAR AND OBSTACLES VANISH.

John Quincy Adams

Conquer your doubt

ACT AS IF WHAT YOU DO MAKES A DIFFERENCE. IT DOES.

William James

FAILURE IS SIMPLY THE OPPORTUNITY TO BEGIN AGAIN, THIS TIME MORE INTELLIGENTLY.

Henry Ford

NEVER GIVE UP, FOR THAT IS JUST THE PLACE AND TIME THAT THE TIDE WILL TURN.

Harriet Beecher Stowe

Inhale the
future; exhale
the past

YOU ARE NEVER TOO OLD TO SET ANOTHER GOAL OR TO DREAM A NEW DREAM.

Les Brown

IF ANYTHING IS WORTH DOING, DO IT WITH ALL YOUR HEART.

Buddha

Pick yourself up
and try again

POSITIVE ANYTHING IS BETTER THAN NEGATIVE NOTHING.

Elbert Hubbard

BE BOLD, BE BOLD, AND EVERYWHERE BE BOLD.

Edmund Spenser

NEVER GIVE IN. NEVER GIVE IN. NEVER, NEVER, NEVER, NEVER — IN NOTHING, GREAT OR SMALL, LARGE OR PETTY, NEVER GIVE IN.

Winston Churchill

Believe in
yourself

YOU CAN, YOU SHOULD, AND IF YOU'RE BRAVE ENOUGH TO START, YOU WILL.

Stephen King

SOME PEOPLE GRUMBLE THAT ROSES HAVE THORNS; I AM GRATEFUL THAT THORNS HAVE ROSES.

Anonymous

To try is to
succeed

ALL LIFE IS AN EXPERIMENT. THE MORE EXPERIMENTS YOU MAKE THE BETTER.

Ralph Waldo Emerson

THE BRAVE MAN IS NOT HE WHO DOES NOT FEEL AFRAID, BUT HE WHO CONQUERS THAT FEAR.

Nelson Mandela

THOUGHTS BECOME THINGS... CHOOSE THE GOOD ONES!

Mike Dooley

There are
no limits

IT IS ONLY BY BEING BOLD THAT YOU GET ANYWHERE.

Richard Branson

THE MORE WE DO, THE MORE WE CAN DO.

William Hazlitt

Have confidence in your decisions

FOLLOW YOUR DREAMS.
THEY KNOW THE WAY.

Kobi Yamada

A JOURNEY OF A THOUSAND MILES BEGINS WITH A SINGLE STEP.

Lao Tzu

THINK BIG THOUGHTS BUT RELISH SMALL PLEASURES.

H. Jackson Brown Jr

Live in the
moment

SUCCESS DOESN'T COME TO YOU; YOU GO TO IT.

T. Scott McLeod

IF THERE IS A GOOD WILL,
THERE IS GREAT WAY.

William Shakespeare

Be your best

WE FALL FORWARD
TO SUCCEED.

Mary Kay Ash

LIVE YOUR LIFE, SING YOUR SONG. NOT FULL OF EXPECTATIONS. NOT FOR THE OVATIONS. BUT FOR THE JOY OF IT.

Rasheed Ogunlaru

SELF-CONFIDENCE AND SELF-COURAGE ARE YOUR GREATEST STRENGTHS.

Lailah Gifty Akita

Seize the day

ENERGY AND PERSISTENCE CONQUER ALL THINGS.

Benjamin Franklin

EXPECT PROBLEMS AND EAT THEM FOR BREAKFAST.

Alfred A. Montapert

Count blessings,
not blows

DON'T GIVE IN TO YOUR FEARS... IF YOU DO, YOU WON'T BE ABLE TO TALK TO YOUR HEART.

Paulo Coelho

THOSE WHO WISH TO SING ALWAYS FIND A SONG.

Swedish proverb

ONCE WE ACCEPT OUR LIMITS, WE GO BEYOND THEM.

Albert Einstein

The higher
you jump, the
closer you get

YOUR PAST IS NOT
YOUR POTENTIAL.

Barbara Winter

OPTIMISM IS THE FAITH THAT LEADS TO ACHIEVEMENT; NOTHING CAN BE DONE WITHOUT HOPE.

Helen Keller

Be open to
the unknown

**MOTIVATION IS INTERNAL.
IT HAS TO COME FROM
WITHIN YOU. DO NOT SEEK
IT ANYWHERE ELSE.**

Abhishek Ratna

THE STRONGEST STEEL
IS FORGED IN THE
HOTTEST FIRE.

Proverb

BEGIN, BE BOLD AND VENTURE TO BE WISE.

Horace

Listen to
the song in
your heart

COMMITMENT LEADS TO ACTION. ACTION BRINGS YOUR DREAM CLOSER.

Marcia Wieder

FAILURES ARE LIKE SKINNED KNEES: PAINFUL BUT SUPERFICIAL.

Ross Perot

Be bold,
be brave,
be yourself

DOUBT WHOM YOU WILL,
BUT NEVER YOURSELF.

Christian Nestell Bovee

EVERY ARTIST WAS
FIRST AN AMATEUR.

Ralph Waldo Emerson

FORTUNE FAVOURS THE PREPARED MIND.

Louis Pasteur

Dare to be different and original

NOTHING IS A WASTE OF TIME IF YOU USE THE EXPERIENCE WISELY.

Auguste Rodin

LUCK IS NOT AS RANDOM AS YOU THINK. BEFORE THAT LOTTERY TICKET WON THE JACKPOT, SOMEONE HAD TO BUY IT.

Vera Nazarian

There is no better time than right now

THE MOST COURAGEOUS ACT IS STILL TO THINK FOR YOURSELF.

Coco Chanel

YOU CANNOT FIND PEACE
BY AVOIDING LIFE.

Michael Cunningham

FREEDOM LIES IN BEING BOLD.

Robert Frost

*Stop existing
and
start living*

**PEOPLE WHO CAN CHANGE
AND CHANGE AGAIN ARE
SO MUCH MORE RELIABLE
AND HAPPIER THAN
THOSE WHO CAN'T.**

Stephen Fry

LIFE SHRINKS OR EXPANDS ACCORDING TO ONE'S COURAGE.

Anaïs Nin

You will achieve your goal

MAKE BOLD CHOICES AND MAKE MISTAKES. IT'S ALL THOSE THINGS THAT ADD UP TO THE PERSON YOU BECOME.

Angelina Jolie

ALWAYS DO WHAT YOU ARE AFRAID TO DO.

Ralph Waldo Emerson

IT DOES NOT MATTER HOW SLOWLY YOU GO AS LONG AS YOU DO NOT STOP.

Confucius

Get up and
get going

THROW CAUTION TO THE WIND AND JUST DO IT.

Carrie Underwood

THE MAN WHO REMOVES A MOUNTAIN BEGINS BY CARRYING AWAY SMALL STONES.

Chinese proverb

You are
extraordinary

SUCCESS IS A SCIENCE; IF YOU HAVE THE CONDITIONS, YOU GET THE RESULT.

Oscar Wilde

IT IS TODAY THAT WE MUST CREATE THE WORLD OF THE FUTURE.

Eleanor Roosevelt

FOLLOW YOUR INNER MOONLIGHT; DON'T HIDE THE MADNESS.

Allen Ginsberg

Why not do it now?

IF YOU WANT TO HAVE THE TIME OF YOUR LIFE, CHANGE HOW YOU USE THE TIME IN YOUR LIFE.

Tim Fargo

YOU CANNOT CHANGE WHAT YOU ARE, ONLY WHAT YOU DO.

Philip Pullman

*Fight fear,
find freedom*

THERE IS ALWAYS
ROOM AT THE TOP.

Daniel Webster

FIND OUT WHO YOU ARE.
AND DO IT ON PURPOSE.

Dolly Parton

YOU ARE NOT STUCK WHERE YOU ARE UNLESS YOU DECIDE TO BE.

Wayne W. Dyer

Take the first
step to success

WE MUST NOT ALLOW OTHER PEOPLE'S LIMITED PERCEPTIONS TO DEFINE US.

Virginia Satir

IF YOU CAN DREAM IT, YOU CAN DO IT.

Tom Fitzgerald

Keep asking
until you get
the answer

THE SWEETEST PLEASURES ARE THOSE WHICH ARE HARDEST TO BE WON.

Giacomo Casanova

FOR MYSELF I AM AN OPTIMIST — IT DOES NOT SEEM TO BE MUCH USE BEING ANYTHING ELSE.

Winston Churchill

PERSEVERANCE IS FAILING NINETEEN TIMES AND SUCCEEDING THE TWENTIETH.

Julie Andrews

Learn to
laugh in the
face of fear

THERE'S NOTHING MORE INTOXICATING THAN DOING BIG, BOLD THINGS.

Jason Kilar

SCARED IS WHAT YOU'RE FEELING... BRAVE IS WHAT YOU'RE DOING.

Emma Donoghue

Live
audaciously

DON'T BE SATISFIED WITH STORIES, HOW THINGS HAVE GONE WITH OTHERS. UNFOLD YOUR OWN MYTH.

Rumi

COURAGE IS FOUND IN UNLIKELY PLACES.

J. R. R. Tolkien

THE ONE THING THAT DOESN'T ABIDE BY MAJORITY RULE IS A PERSON'S CONSCIENCE.

Harper Lee

The higher the
mountain, the
better the view
from the top

BELIEVE YOU CAN AND YOU'RE HALFWAY THERE.

Theodore Roosevelt

THIS LIFE IS WHAT YOU MAKE IT.

Marilyn Monroe

Dare to disturb
the status quo

AT THE END OF THE DAY, LET THERE BE NO EXCUSES, NO EXPLANATIONS, NO REGRETS.

Steve Maraboli

IF YOU DON'T LIKE SOMETHING, CHANGE IT. IF YOU CAN'T CHANGE IT, CHANGE YOUR ATTITUDE. DON'T COMPLAIN.

Maya Angelou

A WISE MAN WILL MAKE MORE OPPORTUNITIES THAN HE FINDS.

Francis Bacon

Be bigger,
be better and
be bolder

IF YOU CAN FIND A PATH WITH NO OBSTACLES, IT PROBABLY DOESN'T LEAD ANYWHERE.

Frank A. Clark

NO GREAT THING IS CREATED SUDDENLY.

Epictetus

You can
and you will

DON'T DIG UP IN DOUBT WHAT YOU PLANTED IN FAITH.

Elisabeth Elliot

LIVE LIFE BIG, BOLD
AND OUT LOUD!

Shannon L. Alder

TURN YOUR FEARS INTO EXCITEMENT. YOUR ANXIETIES INTO ENTHUSIASM. YOUR PASSION INTO ENERGY.

Sanober Khan

Play the game
of life with a
bold spirit and
an open heart

OPPORTUNITY DANCES WITH THOSE WHO ARE ALREADY ON THE DANCE FLOOR.

H. Jackson Brown Jr

TO BE BOLD IS TO BE WISE ENOUGH TO REALISE THAT FEAR IS THE ENERGY THAT FUELS ACTION.

Craig D. Lounsbrough

What are you
waiting for?

FALL SEVEN TIMES AND STAND UP EIGHT.

Japanese proverb

YOUR LIFE IS A BOOK;
MAKE IT A BESTSELLER.

Shanon Grey

EVERYTHING IS PHENOMENAL; EVERYTHING IS INCREDIBLE; NEVER TREAT LIFE CASUALLY.

Abraham Joshua Heschel

Never
give up

ASK FOR WHAT YOU WANT AND BE PREPARED TO GET IT.

Maya Angelou

SHOOT FOR THE MOON.
EVEN IF YOU MISS, YOU'LL
LAND AMONG THE STARS.

Les Brown

Stop making excuses and start making it happen

BOLDNESS
BE MY FRIEND!

William Shakespeare

A BLANK PAGE AND TIME IGNITE INFINITE POSSIBILITIES IN A MIND UNYIELDING TO BOUNDARIES.

Adrienne Dionne

EITHER YOU RUN THE DAY
OR THE DAY RUNS YOU.

Jim Rohn

Remind yourself
how much this
means to you

THE SECRET OF GETTING AHEAD IS GETTING STARTED.

Mark Twain

NO GREAT DISCOVERY
WAS EVER MADE WITHOUT
A BOLD GUESS.

Isaac Newton

Be a little bit
better than you
were yesterday

LIVE DARINGLY, BOLDLY, FEARLESSLY. TASTE THE RELISH TO BE FOUND IN COMPETITION — IN HAVING PUT FORTH THE BEST WITHIN YOU.

Henry J. Kaiser

TELL ME, WHAT IS IT YOU PLAN TO DO WITH YOUR ONE WILD AND PRECIOUS LIFE?

Mary Oliver

DON'T LET THE FEAR
OF FALLING KEEP YOU
FROM CLIMBING UP.

Constance Chuks Friday

Failure is not
an option

A HAPPY LIFE CONSISTS NOT IN THE ABSENCE, BUT IN THE MASTERY OF HARDSHIPS.

Helen Keller

FEAR, TO A GREAT EXTENT, IS BORN OF A STORY WE TELL OURSELVES.

Cheryl Strayed

The future is yours to create

MAKE EACH DAY BOTH USEFUL AND PLEASANT, AND PROVE THAT YOU UNDERSTAND THE WORTH OF TIME BY EMPLOYING IT WELL.

Louisa May Alcott

BE BRAVE ENOUGH TO
BE YOUR TRUE SELF.

Queen Latifah

MOTIVATION IS WHAT GETS YOU STARTED. HABIT IS WHAT KEEPS YOU GOING.

Jim Ryun

Push the boundaries, break the rules and live your life

IN THE MIDDLE OF DIFFICULTY LIES OPPORTUNITY.

Albert Einstein

YOU MUST LEARN A NEW WAY TO THINK BEFORE YOU CAN MASTER A NEW WAY TO BE.

Marianne Williamson

It's never
too late

WE CANNOT BECOME
WHAT WE NEED TO BE BY
REMAINING WHAT WE ARE.

Max De Pree

A SELF THAT GOES ON CHANGING IS A SELF THAT GOES ON LIVING.

Virginia Woolf

THE MAN ON TOP OF THE MOUNTAIN DIDN'T FALL THERE.

Vince Lombardi

Embrace the unknown

TO BE YOURSELF IN A WORLD THAT IS CONSTANTLY TRYING TO MAKE YOU SOMETHING ELSE IS THE GREATEST ACCOMPLISHMENT.

Ralph Waldo Emerson

BE BOLD OR *ITALIC.*
NEVER JUST REGULAR.

Anonymous

*Trust your
instincts*

CHANGE YOUR THOUGHTS AND YOU CHANGE YOUR WORLD.

Norman Vincent Peale

WE ARE AS INDESTRUCTIBLE AS WE BELIEVE OURSELVES TO BE.

John Green

You are
enough

FORTUNE FAVOURS THE BOLD.

Virgil

José is a fun-loving, free-wheeling owl who believes in seizing the day and the power of self-belief! He travels the world, spreading cheer and positivity through his uplifting books.

For more information about our books, find us on Facebook at **Summersdale Publishers** and follow us on Twitter at **@Summersdale**.

www.summersdale.com